Exercise your curiosity with

101

SCIENCE EXPERIMENTS

First published in 2017 by

**Om
KIDZ**
An imprint of Om Books International

Corporate & Editorial Office
A 12, Sector 64, Noida 201 301
Uttar Pradesh, India
Phone: +91 120 477 4100
Email: editorial@ombooks.com
Website: www.ombooksinternational.com

Sales Office
107, Ansari Road, Darya Ganj, New Delhi 110 002, India
Phone: +91 11 40009000
Fax: +91 11 2327 8091
Email: sales@ombooks.com
Website: www.ombooks.com

ISBN: 9789386316127

Printed in India

10 9 8 7 6 5 4 3 2 1

Exercise your curiosity with

101 SCIENCE EXPERIMENTS

Om
KIDZ
An imprint of Om Books International

CONTENTS

KABOOM
EXPERIMENTS THAT INVOLVE
EXPLOSIVE REACTIONS

REACTIONARY
EXPERIMENTS THAT INVOLVE
CHEMICAL REACTIONS

ICKY GOOEY SQUISHY
EXPERIMENTS THAT ARE
EVERY PARENT'S NIGHTMARE

WHAT'S COOKING
EXPERIMENTS WITH
KITCHEN MATERIAL

MAGNETIC MAGIC
EXPERIMENTS ON THE
PRINCIPLE OF MAGNETISM

GETTING HOT IN HERE
EXPERIMENTS ON THE
PRINCIPLE OF HEAT

ALL FALL DOWN
EXPERIMENTS ON THE
PRINCIPLE OF GRAVITY

RELAX DON'T BE DENSE
EXPERIMENTS ON THE
PRINCIPLE OF DENSITY

LET THERE BE LIGHT
EXPERIMENTS ON THE
PRINCIPLE OF LIGHT

SOUND EFFECTS
EXPERIMENTS ON THE
PRINCIPLE OF SOUND

THE AIRY GODMOTHER
EXPERIMENTS ON THE
PRINCIPLE OF AIR

UNDER PRESSURE
EXPERIMENTS ON THE
PRINCIPLE OF AIR PRESSURE

GO GREEN
EXPERIMENTS WITH PLANTS

LIVE IT UP
EXPERIMENTS ON THE HUMAN BODY

GOT YOU
SCIENCE TRICKS AND PRANKS

HIGH AND DRY
EXPERIMENTS WITH WATER

SHOCKING
EXPERIMENTS ON THE PRINCIPLE OF STATIC ELECTRICITY

CURRENT AFFAIRS
EXPERIMENTS ON THE PRINCIPLE OF ELECTRICITY

MISCELLANEOUS EXPERIMENTS

GENERAL GUIDELINES

1. Do not eat food, drink beverages, or chew gum while conducting experiments.
2. Follow all written and verbal instructions carefully. If you do not understand a direction or part of a procedure, ASK AN ELDER BEFORE PROCEEDING WITH THE ACTIVITY.
3. Never conduct experiments without adult supervision.
4. When first entering a science room, do not touch any equipment, chemicals, or other material until you are instructed to do so.
5. Don't play or disturb others while conducting experiments. It can be dangerous.
6. Observe good housekeeping practices. Work areas should be kept clean and tidy at all times.
7. Always work in a well-ventilated area.
8. Be alert and proceed with caution at all times while conducting experiments. Notify an elder immediately of any unsafe conditions you observe.
9. Dispose of all chemical waste properly. Never mix chemicals in sink drains. Sinks are to be used only for water. Check with elders for disposal of chemicals and solutions.
10. Read all labels and equipment instructions carefully before use. Set up and use the equipment as directed by your parent or teacher.
11. Keep hands away from face, eyes, mouth, and body while using chemicals or lab equipment. Wash your hands with soap and water after performing all experiments.
12. Monitor all experiments personally at all times. Do not wander around the room, distract others, or interfere with the laboratory experiments of others.
13. Be aware of the locations and operating procedures of all safety equipment including: first aid kit(s) and fire extinguisher. Know where the fire alarm and the exits are located.

CLOTHING

1. Always wear safety goggles while using chemicals, heat or glassware.
2. Avoid wearing contact lenses while conducting experiments.
3. Dress properly during an experiment. Long hair, dangling jewelry, and loose or baggy clothing are a hazard. Tie long hair. Avoid wearing dangling jewelry and loose clothing.
4. Wear a lab coat or smock during experiments.
5. Wear correct protective gear while conducting experiments.

ACCIDENTS AND INJURIES

1. Report all incidents and injuries immediately.
2. Report any accident (spill, breakage, etc.) or injury (cut, burn, etc.) to your parent/teacher immediately, no matter how trivial it seems. Do not panic.
3. If you are hurt, call someone immediately (and loudly). Do not panic.
4. If a chemical should splash in your eye(s) or on your skin, immediately flush with running water for at least 20 minutes.

HANDLING CHEMICALS

1. Working with chemicals can be dangerous. Avoid handling chemicals with fingers. Always use tweezers. When making an observation, keep at least 1 foot away from the specimen. Do not taste or smell any chemicals.
2. Check the label on all chemical bottles twice before removing any of the contents. Take only as much chemical as you need.
3. Never return unused chemicals to their original container.

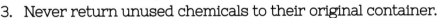

LAB SAFETY

HANDLING GLASSWARE AND EQUIPMENT

1. Be careful in handling glassware and electricity.
2. Never handle broken glass with your bare hands. Use a brush and dustpan to clean up broken glass. Place broken glass in the designated glass disposal container.
3. Examine glassware before each use. Never use chipped, cracked, or dirty glassware.
4. If you do not understand how to use a piece of equipment, ASK THE TEACHER OR YOUR PARENTS FOR HELP!
5. Do not immerse hot glassware in cold water. The glassware may shatter.

HEATING SUBSTANCES

1. Use tongs or heat protective gloves to pick up heated glassware.
2. Do not operate a hot plate by yourself. Take care that hair, clothing, and hands are at a safe distance from the hot plate at all times. Use of hot plate is only allowed in the presence of an elder.
3. Heated glassware remains very hot for a long time. Set them aside in a designated place to cool, and pick up with caution. Use tongs or heat protective gloves if necessary.
4. Never look into a container that is being heated.
5. Do not place hot apparatus directly on the table or desk. Always use an insulated pad. Allow plenty of time for hot apparatus to cool before touching it.

ICONIC ENCOUNTERS

Adult Supervision This icon indicates that parental supervision is required. Always have an adult beside you.

NOTE: All activities and experiments described in this book should be ideally performed with adult supervision. Parents and guardians are advised to oversee the children and assist them with any difficult or potentially harmful tools. Common sense and discretion are advised. The publisher does not assume any responsibility for any injuries or damages arising from any activities.

Tsp – teaspoon

Tbsp – tablespoon

ml – millilitre

l – litre

g – gram

1 cup – 250 ml

Have you ever met two people who just can't get along with each other? Chemical substances are quite the same. Sometimes they blend together perfectly well and create a third substance altogether, but occasionally, they just can't get along, and KABOOM! You have an explosion on your hands. Let's try out some harmless chemical explosions. But remember, chemicals can be dangerous. Make sure an adult is present for all these experiments.

Experiments that involve EXPLOSIVE **Reactions**

01 Elephant's Toothpaste

Duration of experiment

10 Mins

Difficulty level

Medium

What would you need?

Dishwashing liquid

Small cup

¼ cup hydrogen peroxide liquid

1 tbsp. dry yeast

8 drops blue food colouring

3 tbsp. warm water

Plastic bottle

What to do?

Step 1. Pour the hydrogen peroxide into the bottle.

- - - - - - - - - - - - - - -

Step 2. Add the food colouring.

- - - - - - - - - - - - - - -

Step 3. Add the dishwashing liquid and mix it.

- - - - - - - - - - - - - - -

Step 4. Separately, mix the warm water and dry yeast in the cup.

- - - - - - - - - - - - - - -

Step 5. Pour this in the bottle and enjoy the foam.

- - - - - - - - - - - - - - -

What just happened?

The yeast helped to remove the oxygen from the hydrogen peroxide. Since it did this very fast, it created lots and lots of bubbles.

02 Smoky Snake

Duration
of experiment
10 Mins

Difficulty
level
High

What would you need?

Protective eyewear and gloves

Strong glass

Sulphuric acid

Sugar

What to do?

Step 1. Wear protective eyewear and gloves.

- - - - - - - - - - - - - - -

Step 2. Put the sugar in the strong glass.

- - - - - - - - - - - - - - -

Step 3. Add the sulphuric acid to the glass and stir well.

- - - - - - - - - - - - - - -

Step 4. Wait for around 10 minutes and watch a smoky snake rise out of the glass!

- - - - - - - - - - - - - - -

This reaction creates a lot of heat, so be careful while handling the glass.

What just happened?

The water from the sugar got sucked up by the acid and formed carbon. This carbon, along with water vapour, is what you saw as the snake.

03 Volcano in a cup

What would you need?

Wax candle

Fireproof glass container

Cold water

Sand

What to do?

Step 1. Put some wax at the bottom of the container.

Step 2. Fill about half the container with sand.

Step 3. Fill the rest with cold water.

Step 4. Heat the container and wait a while for your waxy explosion to take place.

What just happened?

Just like in a real volcano, once the wax melted, the pressure increased. It found a weak spot in the sand and burst out from there, looking like an actual volcanic eruption.

Duration
of experiment
10 Mins

Difficulty
level
Medium

Duration
of experiment
10 Mins

Difficulty
level
Medium

04 Volcano Vesuvius

What would you need?

Container | ½ cup cooking vinegar | Plastic bottle

2 tsp. baking soda | Clay | 5 drops red food colouring

What to do?

Step 1. Pat some clay around the plastic bottle in the shape of a volcano. You can paint it brown and paint some trees on it to make it look more realistic.

Step 2. Put the baking soda in the bottle.

Step 3. Separately, pour the cooking vinegar into the container till it is half full. Mix the food colouring with this.

Step 4. Then, pour this mixture into the bottle. Watch as your volcano erupts in your room!

What just happened?

The baking soda and cooking vinegar react to form carbonic acid, which is an unstable substance. It breaks apart into water and carbon dioxide, creating all the fizz.

Science around us

Why do volcanoes erupt?

The layer just below the surface of the Earth is known as the 'mantle'. Sometimes, certain conditions cause the mantle to get heated and become liquid. When the pressure is high enough, this liquid searches for weak spots on the Earth's surface and shoots out in the form of red, hot lava.

05 Bag Bomb

Duration of experiment
10 Mins

Difficulty level
Medium

What would you need?

Tissue paper   Zip lock bag   3 tsp. baking soda

½ cup cooking vinegar   ¼ cup warm water

What to do?

Step 1. Pour the warm water into the zip lock bag. Add the cooking vinegar.

Step 2. Wrap the baking soda in the tissue paper.

Step 3. Close half the zip lock bag. Through the open half, put the tissue paper in the bag and close it.

Step 4. Put the bag in the sink. Step back. The bag will begin to expand, and finally burst with a bang!

What just happened?

Don't stand too close to the bag.

The baking soda and cooking vinegar create a reaction, which releases carbon dioxide. The carbon dioxide fills the bag till the bag can no longer hold it and it bursts.

Difficulty level
Medium

Duration of experiment
10 Mins

What would you need?

Tea bag   Lighter   Metal tray   Scissors

06 Tea Bag Rocket

Make sure you aren't anywhere near curtains or anything flammable. Try to perform this outdoors if possible.

What to do?

Step 1. Cut the top of the tea bag.

Step 2. Pour the tea leaves out.

Step 3. Open the bag so that it forms a cylinder.

Step 4. Place it on the tray.

Step 5. Use the lighter to light the top of the tea bag.

What just happened?

Lighting the tea bag caused the air inside to heat up. We all know that hot air rises. The tea bag was light enough for the air to lift along with it.

Unlike the angry substances in the previous section, most substances are rather docile and get along with each other just fine. In this section, you will encounter several chemicals that react with each other to form another substance.

Though most of the experiments are less volatile than those in the previous section, remember that fire can be dangerous. Always have an adult around whenever you are trying to perform any experiment that includes fire.

REACTIONARY

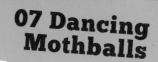

Experiments that involve CHEMICAL **Reactions**

07 Dancing Mothballs

What would you need?

Mothballs   Water   Glass

½ cup cooking vinegar

2 tsp. baking soda

Difficulty
level
Medium

Duration
of experiment
15 Mins

What to do?

Step 1. Dissolve the baking soda in a glass of water.

- - - - - - - - - - - - - - - - - -

Step 2. Add the cooking vinegar.

- - - - - - - - - - - - - - - - - -

Step 3. Put the mothballs in the glass.

- - - - - - - - - - - - - - - - - -

Step 4. Watch the mothballs rise to the surface and sink down again.

- - - - - - - - - - - - - - - - - -

What just happened?

The reaction between cooking vinegar and baking soda created carbon dioxide gas. This gas stuck to the mothballs and made them float on the water. The gas was released into the air, and the mothballs sank down again.

Duration
of experiment
05 Mins

Difficulty
level
High

What would you need?

Tray

35 mm film canister

3 tbsp. water

1 Antacid tablet

What to do?

Step 1. Find a large, open space.

Step 2. Remove the lid of the canister and put the water in it.

Step 3. Quickly put the tablet in the canister and seal it tight with the lid.

Step 4. Immediately put the canister down with the lid on the tray.

Step 5. After about 10 seconds, the film canister will launch into the air.

Stay far away from the rocket.

What just happened?

The water and Antacid reacted to form carbon dioxide.
This increased the pressure in the canister.
The pressure built up till the rocket blasted.
This system of thrust is how a real rocket works,
whether it is in outer space or here in the Earth's atmosphere.

Duration
of experiment
10 Mins

Difficulty
level
Low

What would you need?

Iodine solution

Potato

Plate

Water

What to do?

Step 1. Boil and mash the potato.

Step 2. Put this on a plate and put two drops of iodine on the potato.

Step 3. Watch the iodine solution change from a brown to a purple blue colour.

What just happened?

Potato contains a certain chemical called 'starch'. When this starch is in the presence of iodine, it turns blue.

Duration
of experiment
40 Mins

Difficulty
level
Medium

What would you need?

Test tube   Water

Steel wool   Container

2 tsp. cooking vinegar

What to do?

Step 1. Dip the steel wool in a mixture of vinegar and water.

Step 2. Put some steel wool in the test tube.

Step 3. Fill the container with water.

Step 4. Invert the test tube and place it in the container.

Step 5. Leave your apparatus untouched for two days. You will see the steel wool rust and the water level in the test tube rise.

What just happened?

The vinegar helped speed up the process of rusting. This used up oxygen. As the oxygen in the air was being used up, the air pressure decreased and the water was sucked into the tube.

Science around us

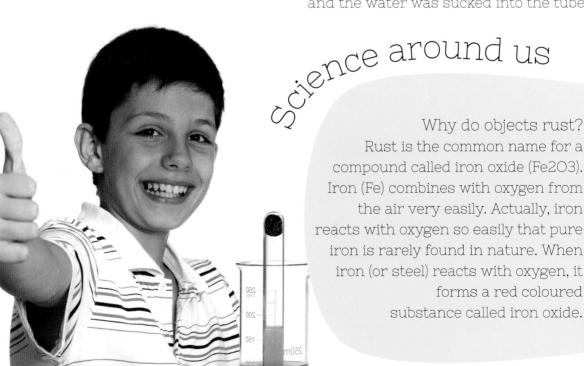

Why do objects rust? Rust is the common name for a compound called iron oxide (Fe_2O_3). Iron (Fe) combines with oxygen from the air very easily. Actually, iron reacts with oxygen so easily that pure iron is rarely found in nature. When iron (or steel) reacts with oxygen, it forms a red coloured substance called iron oxide.

ICKY GOOEY SQUISHY

Experiments
that are every parent's
Nightmare

By the end of this section, you will have made all sorts of icky things like fake snot, fake puke and fake slime. You will also have your very own mouldy orange. But try not to make too much of a mess while making these things, or you may also end up being grounded for two weeks!

Go on... get started... if you dare...

What would you need?

Bowl

6 drops food colouring

¼ cup liquid starch

¼ cup glue

Spoon

¼ cup water

Duration
of experiment
05 Mins

Difficulty
level
Medium

What just happened?

Glue is made up of tiny strands. The liquid starch helps these strands to stay together, giving it a slimy feel.

11 Make Slime

What to do?

Step 1. Pour all the water into the bowl.

- -

Step 2. Add the glue and mix well.

- -

Step 3. Add food colouring to the mixture.

- -

Step 4. Now add the liquid starch and stir it in.

- -

Step 5. You just made fake slime!

12 Quicksand

Duration of experiment
20 Mins

Difficulty level
Medium

Quicksand
Real quicksand works in a similar manner to the quicksand you are about to make. When normal sand becomes so saturated with water that the friction between the sand is reduced, it becomes quicksand. If you ever get stuck in quicksand, just relax. Your body will soon float up.

What would you need?

1 cup cornflour

Large container

Wooden spoon

½ cup water

What to do?

Step 1. Place the cornflour in the container and slowly add water to it, stirring continuously.

Step 2. Stir till it gets the consistency of honey.

Step 3. Stir it around slowly and it will feel like liquid. But if you try to stir it quickly, it will turn solid.

Step 4. Try dropping something in this mixture when it is solid and watch how it slowly gets swallowed up!

What just happened?

When the thick mixture was stirred quickly, it became solid. The cornflour grains can't slide over each other due to lack of water between them. When you stirred slowly, you allowed more water between the cornflour grains, letting them slide over each other more easily.

13 Milk Plastic

Duration of experiment
02 Days

Difficulty level
Medium

What would you need?

1 tbsp. cooking vinegar

Strainer

Cup

Cutters

Warm milk

What to do?

Step 1. Put a tablespoon of cooking vinegar in a cup of warm milk and stir it well.

Step 2. Pour the milk through the strainer. You should be left with a white lumpy solid.

Step 3. Wait for it to cool. Press it into any shape you like and let it dry for a couple of days.

What just happened?

You made a protein called 'casein'. This protein in the milk reacted with the acid in the vinegar and formed lumps, which were easy to mould.

Duration of experiment
12 Mins

Difficulty level
Medium

14 Crazy Putty

What would you need?

1 tsp. borax

Container

Spoon

Glue

Water

What to do?

Step 1. Fill the bottom of the container with glue.

Step 2. Add the same amount of water and stir.

Step 3. Add borax. Stir the mixture.

Step 4. It will soon join together, acting like putty!

What just happened?

When the glue and the borax are combined in a water solution, they react. This creates one giant molecule. The new compound can absorb large amounts of water, producing a putty like substance that you can squish in your hands or even bounce.

Duration
of experiment
48 Hours

Difficulty
level
Medium

15 Paper Mache Pots

What to do?

Step 1. Tear the newspaper into very small pieces and soak them in the container in hot water overnight.

- -

Step 2. Drain out the excess water and mash the paper using a potato masher.

- -

Step 3. Once it achieves a pulpy, liquid consistency, fill it in the yoghurt cup.

- -

Step 4. Remove it from the cup and pour it into a sieve. Drain out the excess water.

- -

Step 5. Coat the sides of the yoghurt cup with the drained pulp and put it on a window sill to dry.

- -

Step 6. Remove it from the cup after two days.

- -

Step 7. Paint it to look pretty. You can now grow your own plant in the pot!

- -

What would you need?

Sieve

Yoghurt cup

Potato masher

Newspaper

Large container

Hot water

What just happened?

The water is absorbed by the pulp, making it easier to reshape. The pulp pots maintain their new shape even after drying.

WHAT'S COOKING?

Do you know that many items from your kitchen can actually be used as substitute chemicals in science experiments? There is science in just about everything around us. I bet you didn't know that you could actually make an electric battery using a lemon. In this section, you can find out how. Just make sure you tell your parents when you finish all the vinegar in the house, unless you want to run an errand and buy more!

Experiments with Kitchen Material

16 Colour Symphony

What would you need?

Food colouring

Tray

Whole milk

5 drops dishwashing soap

Duration
of experiment

05 Mins

Difficulty
level

Low

What to do?

Step 1. Pour a thin layer of milk onto the tray.

Step 2. Add six drops of different coloured food colouring onto the milk in different spots.

Step 3. Add the dishwashing soap onto the drops of food colouring.

Step 4. Watch the colours go berserk.

What just happened?

Soap breaks down fat. The liquid soap in the tray tried to break down the fat in the milk. While it was doing that, it caused the colours to scatter.

Duration
of experiment

10 Mins

Difficulty
level

Low

What would you need?

Raw egg

Water

Candle

Tongs

What to do?

Step 1. Blacken the egg by holding it with tongs over a flame.

Step 2. Put it in the jar of water.

Step 3. See the soot disappear and watch it start to shine.

The carbon in the soot repels the water and holds a thin film of air on the egg's surface. This layer of air under the soot gives the egg a silvery coat.

What just happened?

---

18 Squishy Egg

What would you need?

Raw egg

Large bowl

Cooking vinegar

What just happened?

Vinegar, an acid, dissolves the calcium in the eggshell. Calcium makes the shell hard. But a thin, flexible membrane just under the shell still holds the egg's shape.

Duration
of experiment

07 Days

Difficulty
level

Low

What to do?

Step 1. Put the egg into a bowl and cover it completely with vinegar.

Step 2. Wait for a week and drain the vinegar.

Step 3. You can now play with your rubber egg!

Step 4. Be careful though, don't break the membrane!

19 Fold the Egg

Duration of experiment
01 Week

Difficulty level
High

What would you need?

Glass

Raw egg

Cooking vinegar

Pin

What to do?

Step 1. Make two small holes on both ends of the egg. They should be about half a centimetre in diameter.

- -

Step 2. Poke the pin through one of the holes and jiggle it around so the yolk breaks.

- -

Step 3. Clean one end of the egg and blow into the hole so that all the liquid comes out from the other end. The egg should be completely hollow.

- -

Step 4. Place this hollow egg in a glass full of vinegar and leave it for a week.

- -

Step 5. After a week, squeeze the vinegar out of the egg. It should be soft and flexible now.

- -

Step 5. Fold the egg, it becomes flat! Try tossing and bouncing it around between your hands; it regains its original round shape!

- -

What just happened?

The acetic acid in the vinegar dissolves the calcium in the shell, which causes the shell to lose its hardness. When you fold it, the air exits the membrane through the tiny holes. Tossing it around lets air enter the membrane, allowing it to regain its shape.

What would you need?

Duration
of experiment
15 Mins

Difficulty
level
High

Lime

Small light bulb

Nails

Wire

Electric tape

What to do?

Step 1. Squeeze the lime without breaking its skin.

- - - - - - - - - - - - - - - - - - - -

Step 2. Insert both nails into the fruit at a distance of two inches from each other.

- - - - - - - - - - - - - - - - - - - -

Step 3. Peel the plastic insulation off the bulb (leads of the light).

- - - - - - - - - - - - - - - - - - - -

Step 4. Wrap the wires around the head of the two nails.

- - - - - - - - - - - - - - - - - - - -

Step 5. Secure the wire around the nails using electric tape.

- - - - - - - - - - - - - - - - - - - -

What just happened?

Citric fruits conduct electricity because of their acidic content. The different charges of the lime and the nail cause the electric flow.

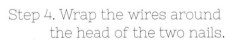

21 Glowing Sugar

What would you need?

Sugar lumps   Pliers

Duration
of experiment
15 Mins

Difficulty
level
Medium

What to do?

Step 1. Take the sugar lumps to a dark room.

- - - - - - - - - - - - - - - -

Step 2. Crush them with the pliers.

- - - - - - - - - - - - - - - -

Step 3. You will be able to see small flashes of blue-green sparks.

- - - - - - - - - - - - - - - -

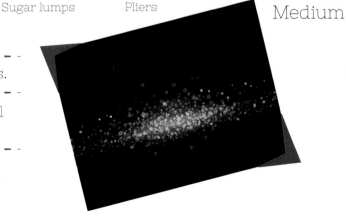

What just happened?

When sugar crystals break, sometimes, one side has more positive charge than the other. When you crush the lumps, you are pulling apart the positive and the negative charges. This gives off enough energy to make it spark.

MAGNETIC MAGIC

Experiments on the principle of *Magnetism*

I bet you must have played with magnets at some point of time. But you probably didn't know that the first magnet was discovered by a poor shepherd boy named Magnes more than three thousand years ago! All magnets have a North Pole and a South Pole. And as they say, opposites attract. This applies to magnets as well. The North Pole of one magnet will be attracted to only the South Pole of another magnet and repelled by its North Pole. Another interesting property of magnets is that the North Pole of a magnet, when suspended freely, always points towards the North!

What would you need?

Paper

Scissors

Paper clip

Magnet

Thread

Tape

Table

Duration
of experiment
05 Mins

Difficulty
level
Low

22 Magnetic Pick Up

What to do?

Step 1. Cut a three inch paper in the shape of a kite. Attach a paper clip to one corner.

- - - - - - - - - - - - - -

Step 2. Tape a piece of thread on the opposite corner.

- - - - - - - - - - - - - -

Step 3. Tape the other end of the thread to a table.

- - - - - - - - - - - - - -

Step 4. Hold the magnet near the paper clip. Watch the kite 'fly'.

- - - - - - - - - - - - - -

What just happened?

Magnets have a magnetic field, an invisible force that attracts some kinds of metal. Metal objects within the magnetic field do not have to touch a magnet to be pulled by magnetism.

23 Find the North

Duration of experiment
15 Mins

Difficulty level
Medium

What would you need?

Magnet

String

Compass

What to do?

Step 1. Tie a loop around the centre of the magnet with the string. Suspend the magnet by holding the string.

Step 2. Wait till it settles in one position.

Step 3. With the help of a compass, see which end of the magnet is pointing North. Mark it 'S'. This is the South Pole of the magnet, which will always be attracted to the North Pole of the Earth.

Step 4. Simply suspend the magnet anytime; 'S' will always point to the North.

What just happened?

One end of every magnet is called the North Pole and the other, the South. The North Pole of the magnet is always attracted to the South Pole of the Earth and vice versa.

Difficulty level
Medium

Duration of experiment
15 Mins

What would you need?

Horseshoe magnet

Clay

Pencil

24 Make a Compass

What just happened?

One end of every magnet is called the North Pole and the other, the South. The North Pole of the magnet is always attracted to the South Pole of the Earth.

What to do?

Step 1. Mould the clay to form a mound.

Step 2. Stick the pencil into this mound with the pointy end on top.

Step 2. Balance the magnet on the pointy end and let it settle in the north-south direction.

25 Fun with Magnets

Duration of experiment
10 Mins

Difficulty level
Low

What would you need?

Salt

Chalk

Paper clips

Plastic bottle

Magnet

What to do?

Step 1. Add an equal amount of coloured chalk powder and salt in a bottle.

- - - - - - - - - - - - - - - - - -

Step 2. Add the paper clips and shake the bottle.

- - - - - - - - - - - - - - - - - -

Step 3. Hold up a magnet to the bottle and watch the paper clips jump up towards the magnet!

- - - - - - - - - - - - - - - - - -

What just happened?

The metallic objects were attracted to the magnet, but the salt and chalk were not. Only metals are attracted to magnets. That is why the clips 'jumped' out through the salt and chalk.

What would you need?

Paper clips   Paper plate   Magnet   Poster paint

26 Make a Magnet Painting

Duration of experiment
15 Mins

Difficulty level
Low

What to do?

Step 1. Squirt different coloured paints onto the plate.

- - - - - - - - - - - - - - - - - -

Step 2. Place the paper clips on the plate.

- - - - - - - - - - - - - - - - - -

Step 3. Hold the magnet under the plate and guide the clip through the paint.

- - - - - - - - - - - - - - - - - -

What just happened?

The paper clip is attracted to the magnet. When you move the magnet, you move the paper clip along with it, creating a metal 'paintbrush'.

What would you need?

Cornflakes

Bowl and spoon

Magnet

White paper

Duration
of experiment

15 Mins

Difficulty
level

Difficult

What to do?

Step 1. Crush the cereal in your bowl with the help of a spoon until it becomes a powder.

Step 2. Pour this powder onto the white paper.

Step 3. Run your magnet over it.

Step 4. You should be able to pick up tiny black particles.

Step 5. These are actually little bits of iron in your cereal!

What just happened?

Iron is a mineral that is necessary for our survival in small proportions. It is also magnetic and so gets picked up with the magnet.

---

28 Car Racing

What would you need?

Toy cars

Magnet

Rubber Bands

Duration
of experiment

15 Mins

Difficulty
level

Medium

What to do?

Step 1. Use the rubber bands to attach one bar magnet under each of the cars.

Step 2. The North Pole should be facing the back of one car and the front of the other.

Step 3. Put the two cars one behind the other and see if you can 'push' the car in front without touching it.

What just happened?

Similar poles of magnets repel each other.

GETTING HOT IN HERE

Experiments on the principle of Heat

Just like you get irritable and cranky when the weather is too hot, heat can have an interesting effect on other substances too. When air is heated, it expands and rises. Though this seems rather unimpressive, this property of air can be used in many fascinating ways, as you will learn in this section. Also learn how to elude the wrath of fire by making fireproof balloons, handkerchiefs and paper vessels! Once again, remember that fire can be very dangerous and adult supervision is strongly recommended for all experiments that involve the use of fire.

29 Fireproof Balloons

Duration of experiment
15 Mins

Difficulty level
Medium

What to do?

Step 1. Put water in a balloon. Inflate and tie it.

Step 2. Inflate the other balloon without the water.

Step 3. Hold a lit matchstick under the balloon that does not have water. It will burst.

Step 4. Now, hold a lit matchstick under the balloon with water. It won't burst.

What would you need?

Balloons

Matchsticks

¼ cup water

What just happened?

The water absorbs most of the heat in the case of the second balloon. This is why the water inside the balloon becomes hot, but the balloon does not burst.

30 Levitating Spiral

Duration of experiment
10 Mins

Difficulty level
Medium

What would you need?

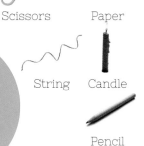

Scissors   Paper

String   Candle

Pencil

What to do?

Step 1. Draw a thin spiral on a piece of paper and cut it out.

Step 2. Light the candle.

Step 3. Tie the spiral to the pencil using the string. Hold this over the candle.

Step 4. Watch as the paper rises by itself.

! Don't hold the spiral too close to the flame. It could catch fire.

What just happened?

The air around the candle gets heated. As the air gets warmer, it expands and becomes lighter. It rises. Since the spiral is light, it rises along with the air.

---

31 The Talking Coin

Duration of experiment
20 Mins

Difficulty level
Low

What would you need?

Plastic bottle   Water   Coin

What to do?

Step 1. Put the empty bottle in the freezer for 15 minutes

Step 2. Wet the coin.

Step 3. Take the bottle out and put it on a table.

Step 4. Quickly put the wet coin over the mouth of the bottle.

Step 5. Watch the coin bob up and down, as if it's talking.

What just happened?

The air in the bottle cooled when it was in the freezer. Cold air contracts and air from outside the bottle moved into the bottle. Outside, the air expanded. Since it had no place to go, it pushed against the coin, making it bob.

Duration of experiment
05 Mins

Difficulty level
Medium

What would you need?

Hot water

Paper towel

2 plastic glasses

What to do?

Step 1. Wet the paper towel with the hot water, but don't crumple it.

Step 2. Fill one of the plastic glasses with hot water and pour it out.

Step 3. Lay the paper on top of this glass.

Step 4. Pour some hot water into the other glass and pour it out.

Step 5. Turn this glass over and put it on top of the paper towel.

Step 5. Hold it there for 30 seconds and pick it up. You will find that both glasses are stuck to each other.

What is heat energy?
Heat energy is the term used to describe the level of activity in the molecules of an object. The Sun is the primary source of heat energy in our solar system.

What just happened?

When you pour the hot water into the glasses, it heats the air inside, which expands. Once the air starts cooling, the pressure reduces, but new air cannot enter the glasses because they are stuck together. The pressure from the air outside keeps the glasses firmly stuck to each other.

You've probably heard of Newton and how he discovered gravity when an apple fell on his head. In this section, you can do your own little experiments to prove his theory. You can also study certain processes that 'defy' gravity, like capillary action and the centrifugal force.

You will also learn how to balance a rather large number of irregularly shaped objects using the principle of 'centre of gravity'.

ALL FALL DOWN

Experiments
on the principle of
Gravity

33 Anti-Gravity Water

Duration of experiment
05 Mins

Difficulty level
Medium

What would you need?

Glass

Cardboard

Water

What to do?

Step 1. Fill the glass to the brim with water.

- - - - - - - - - - - - - - - -

Step 2. Cover it with the cardboard. Make sure that no air bubbles enter the glass.

- - - - - - - - - - - - - - - -

Step 3. Hold the cardboard and turn the glass upside down, preferably over a sink.

- - - - - - - - - - - - - - - -

Step 4. Now move your hand away from the cardboard. The cardboard remains in place, defying gravity.

- - - - - - - - - - - - - - - -

What just happened?
By not allowing any air to enter the glass, you made sure that the air pressure outside the glass was greater than the air pressure inside. This helped keep the cardboard in place.

34 Magical Water

Duration of experiment: 02 Hours

Difficulty level: Low

What to do?

Step 1. Fill two glasses with water.

Step 2. Put blue paint in one and yellow in the other.

Step 3. Place the empty glass between the two.

Step 4. Twist the paper towels together and set them up as shown.

Step 5. You will soon see the empty glass filling up with green water!

What would you need?

Paper towels

Glasses

Yellow and blue paint

Water

What just happened?

By a process called capillary action, the water uses the tiny gaps between the fibres of the paper towels to move along. When the yellow and blue paint mix in the empty glass, it forms green water.

---

35 Dual Coloured Flowers

Duration of experiment: 48 Hours

Difficulty level: Medium

What to do?

Step 1. Slit the stem of the flower vertically with the knife.

Step 2. Mix different coloured inks and water in each glass.

Step 3. Put one half of the stem in one glass and the other half in the other glass.

Step 4. In a few hours, the petals of your flower will appear dual coloured!

What would you need?

White flower · Coloured ink

Knife

Glasses

Water

What just happened?

The water travels up the stem of the plant into the leaves and flowers, where it makes food. This process is called 'capillary action'.

36 Parachute

Duration of experiment
30 Mins

Difficulty level
Medium

What would you need?

Small toy

String

Plastic bag

Scissors

What to do?

Step 1. Cut out an octagon from the plastic bag.

- - - - - - - - - - - - - -

Step 2. Cut a small hole near the edge of each side.

- - - - - - - - - - - - - -

Step 3. Attach eight pieces of equal-sized string to each of the holes.

- - - - - - - - - - - - - -

Step 4. Tie the pieces of string to the toy and drop your parachute slowly.

- - - - - - - - - - - - - -

What just happened?

When you release the parachute, the weight pulls down on the strings and opens up a large surface area of material that uses air resistance to slow it down.

---

37 Anti-Gravity Machine

Duration of experiment
30 Mins

Difficulty level
High

What would you need?

Tape

2 plastic funnels of the same size

Long rulers

Thick books

What to do?

Step 1. Tape the two funnels together and set up the rest of the apparatus as shown in the picture.

- - - - - - - - - - - - - -

Step 2. Place the funnels at the 'bottom' (narrower end) of the slope. Watch as it rolls up towards the higher pile!

- - - - - - - - - - - - - -

What just happened?

Though it seems as if the funnel is climbing the slope, it is actually moving down towards the table, thanks to its centre of gravity.

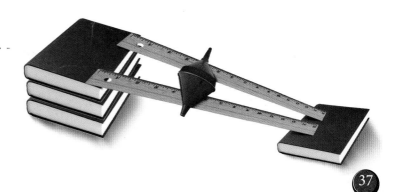

Duration of experiment
30 Mins

Difficulty level
High

What would you need?

Bouncy ball

Knife

Pencil

Paper

Scotch tape

Scissors

What to do?

Step 1. Cut the bouncy ball in half.

Step 2. Place it on a table with the flat side facing up.

Step 3. Draw a 10 cm x 10 cm square on the paper. Cut it out.

Step 4. Roll the square paper to form a tube. Tape it to the cut ball. The round part of the ball should stick out from the bottom.

Step 5. Keep cutting small sections off the top of the paper tube till the tube returns to an upright position when it's knocked over.

Step 6. Draw a clown on the paper tube and play with your toy.

What just happened?

The centre of gravity for an object is the point at which the object's average weight is located. If you support the centre of gravity, you support the entire object. When you cut this ball in half there is a shift in the centre of gravity and the object loses its support, which causes the toy to return to an upright position after being knocked over.

RELAX DON'T BE DENSE!

Have you ever wondered why smaller objects are sometimes heavier than larger objects? The answer lies in their 'density'. Density is the amount of matter that is packed into an object. If a bar of gold is heavier than a piece of wood of the same size, it means that gold is denser than wood.

The next time someone calls you dense, all you need to say for the perfect retort is, "Yes, I'm dense because I have extra brain cells packed in my skull".

Experiments
on the principle of Density

39 Peeling the Orange

What would you need?

2 oranges

Bowl

Water

Duration
of experiment
05 Mins

Difficulty
level
Low

What to do?

Step 1. Fill the bowl with water.

Step 2. Peel one of the oranges.

Step 3. Place both the oranges in the bowl.

Step 4. Contrary to what you think, the orange with the peel floats while the peeled orange sinks.

What just happened?

The peel of the orange is full of tiny air pockets that help give it a lower density than water, making it float to the surface. Removing the peel (and all the air pockets) from the orange increases its density, making it sink. So even though the peeled orange is lighter than the orange with the peel, it sinks.

40 Motion Ocean

Duration of experiment
15 Mins

Difficulty level
Low

What would you need?

 Jar

 Glitter

 Water

 Plastic floating toys

 10 drops food colouring

 Baby oil

What to do?

Step 1. Fill half the jar with water. Add the food colouring and glitter.

Step 2. Add baby oil till 3/4th of the jar is full.

Step 3. Place a floating toy on top of the oil. Screw the lid on.

Step 4. Shake the jar gently to set your ocean in motion.

What just happened?

Water is denser than oil. The two liquids never mix. When the water moves, it pushes the oil around, making shapes like waves.

---

41 Cool Crystals

Duration of experiment
7-8 Days

Difficulty level
Low

What would you need?

 Hot water

 Jar

 Dish

 Paper clips

 Baking soda

 Woollen thread

Spoon

What to do?

Step 1. Fill two jars with hot water.

Step 2. Add baking soda until you can't dissolve any more.

Step 3. Attach paper clips to the ends of the thread.

Step 4. Suspend it in the jars, as shown.

Step 5. Place a dish under the lowest part of the thread. Crystals form in a week.

What just happened?

The baking soda drips off the lowest point of the thread onto the plate. However, a small amount of the baking soda remains on the thread after each drip.

42 Rainbow in a Glass

Duration of experiment: 30 Mins

Difficulty level: High

What would you need?

Vegetable oil

Blue food colouring

Honey

Rubbing alcohol

Water

Glass

Dishwashing liquid

What to do?

Step 1. Fill 1/4th of the glass with honey.

- - - - - - - - - - - - - - - - - - - -

Step 2. Tip the glass slightly and add dishwashing liquid.

- - - - - - - - - - - - - - - - - - - -

Step 3. Mix some food colouring and water and add it to the glass.

- - - - - - - - - - - - - - - - - - - -

Step 4. Add some vegetable oil to the mixture.

- - - - - - - - - - - - - - - - - - - -

Step 5. Finally, add the rubbing alcohol.

- - - - - - - - - - - - - - - - - - - -

What just happened?

Denser liquids settle at the bottom, while the less dense liquids float to the top.

---

43 Bottle Accelerometer

Duration of experiment: 10 Mins

Difficulty level: Low

What would you need?

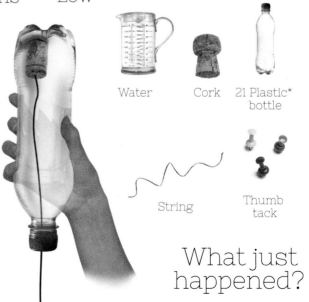

Water

Cork

21 Plastic* bottle

String

Thumb tack

What to do?

Step 1. Attach one end of the string to the cork with the thumb tack.

- - - - - - - - - - - - - - - - - - - -

Step 2. Put this in the bottle of water and screw the cap over the other end of the string.

- - - - - - - - - - - - - - - - - - - -

Step 3. Turn the bottle over and walk around the room. The cork moves in whichever direction you move!

- - - - - - - - - - - - - - - - - - - -

What just happened?

Because water has a greater density, the cork is pushed forward when you walk.

* Bottle type : 21 Plastic bottle

LET THERE BE LIGHT

What's the fastest thing you can think of? A racing car? An aeroplane? They're both nothing compared to the speed of light! Nothing travels faster than light. Light from the sun covers a distance of 150,000,000 kms in around 8 minutes!
In fact, it has been hypothesised that if we could find a way to travel faster than the speed of light, time travel may actually be possible. Sounds cool, doesn't it?

Experiments on the principle of Light

44 Make a Rainbow

Duration of experiment	Difficulty level
10 Mins	Medium

What to do?

Step 1. Fill three quarters of the glass with water.

- - - - - - - - - - - - - - -

Step 2. Take the glass and the paper to your window.

- - - - - - - - - - - - - - -

Step 3. Hold the glass above the paper. Let sunlight pass through the glass and fall on the paper.

- - - - - - - - - - - - - - -

Step 4. Adjust your paper a little till you see a mini rainbow on it.

- - - - - - - - - - - - - - -

What would you need?

Glass

White paper

Water

What just happened?

When sunlight passes through water, it refracts or bends, splitting into seven colours. This is what you just created on your paper.

45 Make Your Own Kaleidoscope

Duration of experiment
20 Mins

Difficulty level
High

What to do?

Step 1. Cut the mirror into three 4 x 15 cm strips using the glass cutter.

- - - - - - - - - - - - - - - - - - - -

Step 2. Cut the cardboard into three similar strips.

- - - - - - - - - - - - - - - - - - - -

Step 3. Paste the cardboard strips on the back of the mirror. Tape the three strips together in the form of a triangle.

- - - - - - - - - - - - - - - - - - - -

Step 4. Look at some sequins through the kaleidoscope and rotate it. Enjoy the colourful display.

What just happened?

Light travels in a straight line. But when it hits the mirror, it is reflected. The reflections bounce back and forth from side to side, creating multiple images.

What would you need?

Cardboard

Sequins

Mirror

Glass cutter

Tape

Ruler

Duration of experiment
12 Hours

Difficulty level
Low

46 Sundial

What to do?

Step 1. Fix the stick vertically into the ground.

- - - - - - - - - - - - - - - - - - - -

Step 2. Every hour, mark where the shadow of the stick is falling. Number the marking depending on the time.

- - - - - - - - - - - - - - - - - - - -

Step 3. To see the time, just look at the shadow and read the corresponding number.

- - - - - - - - - - - - - - - - - - - -

What just happened?

The shadow of the stick depends upon the position of the Sun, which changes every hour.

What would you need?

Watch

Stick

47 Make an Eclipse

Duration of experiment
10 Mins

Difficulty level
Medium

What would you need?

String

Ping-pong ball

Tape

Globe

Lamp

What to do?

Step 1. Attach a piece of string to the ping-pong ball with the tape.

Step 2. Switch on the lamp. Suspend the ball between the lamp and the globe.

Step 3. Notice how the shadow forms on the globe.

What just happened?

The lamp represents the Sun, the ball is the moon and the globe is the Earth. An actual solar eclipse takes place in the same way when the moon comes in between the Sun and the Earth.

---

48 Bend Light

Duration of experiment
10 Mins

Difficulty level
Medium

What would you need?

Shoe box

Scissors

Jar

Water

Torch

What to do?

Step 1. Cut a small slit at one end of the shoe box.

Step 2. Fill the jar with water.

Step 3. Put the jar in the box against the slit.

Step 4. Go to a dark room and shine a torch through the slit.

Step 5. Watch the light 'bend'!

What just happened?

Light 'bends' or refracts because of the different speeds of light in air and water. When light enters water, it bends and does so once again while exiting.

SOUND EFFECTS

Try to imagine a world without sound. You wouldn't be able to listen to music, watch TV or even talk to anyone! Sound travels in waves and needs a medium to travel. Hence, sound can travel through liquids like water, gases like air and solids like wood. Did you know that in space, where there is a vacuum (no air), astronauts cannot speak to each other the way we do? They use walkie talkies and ear pieces to talk to each other when they are not in their capsule!

Experiments
on the principle of
Sound

49 Musical Glasses

What to do?

Step 1. Put all the glasses in a line. Fill the first one with a little water, the second with slightly more and so on.

- - - - - - - - - - - - - - - - -

Step 2. Hit the glass with the least amount of water using a pencil and observe the sound. Then, hit the glass with the most water. Notice the difference in the sound.

- - - - - - - - - - - - - - - - -

Step 3. Enjoy creating a tune!

- - - - - - - - - - - - - - - - -

What would you need?

Water   Glasses   Pencil

What just happened?

Small vibrations are made when you hit the glass; this creates sound waves which travel through the water. More water means slower vibrations and a deeper tone.

Duration	Difficulty
of experiment	level
20 Mins	Medium

50 Jumping Rice

Duration of experiment: 10 Mins

Difficulty level: Low

What would you need?

Rice

Bowl

Pan

Cling wrap

Spoon

Rubber bands

What to do?

Step 1. Stretch the cling wrap over the top of the bowl and secure it with a rubber band.

Step 2. Sprinkle a few grains of rice on top.

Step 3. Hold the pan close and hit it with the spoon to see the rice jump!

What just happened?

Sound travels in the form of waves. The waves travel through the air and hit the cling wrap, making it vibrate. The vibrations cause the rice to jump.

---

51 Roaring Balloon

Duration of experiment: 05 Mins

Difficulty level: Low

What would you need?

Balloon

Coins

What to do?

Step 1. Put a rough edged coin into the empty balloon and blow it up.

Step 2. Swirl the balloon around such that the coin is rolling against the balloon.

Step 3. You should be able to hear your balloon roar!

What just happened?

The edge of the coin is rough and bounces on the balloon's surface. This causes small vibrations. The noise is magnified by the air in the balloon.

Duration
of experiment

10 Mins

Difficulty
level

Low

What would you need?

Scissors

2 tin cans

String

52 Hello

Step 1. Cut a long piece of string (around 6 feet).

Step 2. Make a small hole at the bottom of both cans.

Step 3. Thread the string through each can and tie a knot to secure it.

Step 4. Ask a friend to take one can and stand at a distance that makes the string completely tight.

Step 5. Hold your can to your ear.

Step 6. Ask your friend to talk into hers. Then, exchange places and talk into the can and ask your friend to listen.

What just happened?

Speaking into the can creates sound waves that are converted into vibrations at the bottom of the can. These vibrations travel along the string and are converted back into sound waves.

47

53 Popsicle Stick Harmonica

Duration of experiment
30 Mins

Difficulty level
Medium

What would you need?

Ice-cream sticks

Craft paper
(2 strips about
3 cm × 1 cm)

Tape

Rubber bands

What to do?

Step 1. Put one stick on top of the other.

Step 2. Cut out two strips from the craft paper, about 3 cm x 1 cm each.

Step 3. Tape the strips about 1.5 cm from each end. Make sure that the tape does not touch the sticks at all.

Step 4. Slide the bottom stick out.

Step 5. Stretch a rubber band along the length of the top stick.

Step 6. Place the bottom stick back in its place. The rubber band should go around the top stick only, not the bottom stick as well.

Step 7. Hold the 'harmonica' up to your lips and blow through it.

What just happened?

The air blowing through the rubber band makes it vibrate against the sticks, making the sound.

How do we talk?

The basis of all sounds is vibration. Speech actually starts in the stomach with the diaphragm, which pushes air from the lungs into the voice box. This causes the strings in the voice box to vibrate, creating a sound. The tongue, lips, teeth and roof of the mouth help in shaping the sounds.

54 Dancing Wire

Duration of experiment: 10 Mins

Difficulty level: Medium

What would you need?

Water

Wine glasses

Wire

What to do?

Step 1. Fill less than a quarter of the two wine glasses with the same amount of water. Make them stand at a short distance from each other.

- - - - - - - - - - - - - - - -

Step 2. Place the wire across one of the glasses.

- - - - - - - - - - - - - - - -

Step 3. Wet your finger and rub it over the rim of the first glass.

- - - - - - - - - - - - - - - -

Step 4. The wire on the second glass begins to jump around!

- - - - - - - - - - - - - - - -

What just happened?

This phenomenon, in which an object begins to vibrate because another object in its vicinity is vibrating at the right frequency, is called 'resonance'.

Duration of experiment: 10 Mins

Difficulty level: Medium

55 Musical Buttons

Button   Strings

What would you need?

What to do?

Step 1. Thread the string through one button hole and bring it back up through the other. Tie the ends to form a loop.

- - - - - - - - - - - - - - - -

Step 2. Bring the button to the centre of the string and stretch it out between both your pointer fingers.

- - - - - - - - - - - - - - - -

Step 3 Wind up the string. Pull the string tight and loosen it.

- - - - - - - - - - - - - - - -

What just happened?

The spinning button and the string are vibrating the air around them, making the singing sound.

49

56 Umbrella Speakers

Duration of experiment
30 Mins

Difficulty level
Medium

What would you need?

Watch

Two stands

Nails

Tape

2 umbrellas

What to do?

Step 1. Place two open umbrellas outdoors, around 2.5 metres apart. Their handles should face each other.

Step 2. Use the stand and nails to fix the handles of the umbrellas to the ground with the umbrella placed on the ground such that the handles are parallel to the ground.

Step 3. Place the watch at different spots in the umbrella and notice at which spot the ticking is the loudest. Tape the ticking watch to that spot.

Step 4. Place your ear at the corresponding spot on the other umbrella.

Step 5. You can hear the clock ticking!

What just happened?

The sound waves from the watch are amplified because of the shape of the umbrella. These waves bounce off the first umbrella and hit the other umbrella. The sound then bounces off the corresponding spot on the other umbrella, which is why you can hear it.

UNDER PRESSURE

'Air pressure', as the name rightly suggests, is the pressure constantly exerted by the air that surrounds us. The unit of pressure is 'atmosphere' and is denoted by 'kgf'. There is a pressure of 1 kgf on every square centimetre. This means that a weight of 200 kgf presses down on your hand at every moment!

In fact, the phrase 'as light as air' is technically very misleading because a cubic metre of air weighs about 1.3 kg. The weight of all the air on Earth is 5,000,000,000,000,000,000,000 kg!

Experiments on the principle of Air Pressure

Duration of experiment
20 Mins

Difficulty level
Medium

57 Thirsty Candle

What would you need?

Bowl

Glass

Matchsticks

Candle

Food colouring

Water

Step 1. Fill very little water in the bowl. Add two drops of food colouring to it.

Step 2. Place the candle in the middle of the bowl and light it.

Step 3. Turn the glass over and place it over the candle.

Step 4. Watch as the coloured water gets sucked into the glass.

What just happened?

When the candle burns inside the glass, the air inside the glass expands, creating a higher air pressure. The high pressure air inside tries to move towards the lower pressure air outside, creating space for the water to get 'sucked' in.

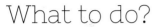

58 Balloon Rocket

Duration of experiment
20 Mins

Difficulty level
Low

What would you need?

Stool

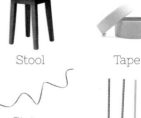
Tape

String

Balloon

Straw

What to do?

Step 1. Tie one end of the string to a chair or stool.

Step 2. Put the other end of the string through the straw.

Step 3. Pull the string tight.

Step 4. Blow up the balloon, pinch the end and tape the balloon to the straw.

Step 5. Let go and watch the rocket fly!

What just happened?

The air rushes out of the balloon, making it move forward. This sort of force is called 'thrust'.

59 The Hungry Bottle

Duration of experiment
10 Mins

Difficulty level
Medium

What would you need?

Matchsticks

Oil

Paper   Banana

Glass bottle

What to do?

Step 1. Tear the paper into small pieces. Dip them in oil.

Step 2. Put these in the bottle.

Step 3. Drop a lit matchstick in the bottle.

Step 4. Quickly place the banana over the bottle with the flesh in the bottle, and the peels at the sides.

Step 5. Watch the bottle eat the banana hungrily!

What just happened?

The burning paper used up all the oxygen in the bottle. This caused a lower pressure in the bottle. The air pressure outside was sufficient to push the banana into the bottle.

What would you need?

Scissors

Rubber band

Tape

Cardboard

Metal wires

Step 1. Tape the straight straws horizontally across the cardboard on opposite ends.

Bendy straw

Bottle cap

Step 2. Push the wire through these straws.

Step 3. Make a hole in the bottle caps and push them into the wire, to create wheels.

Straight straw

Balloon

Step 4. Cut a bendy straw in half.

Step 5. Tie the balloon to one end of this straw with the rubber band.

Step 6. Tape the bendy straw to the cardboard.

Step 7. Blow the balloon through the straw and leave it on a smooth surface to see the car move forward.

What just happened?

After you put the car on a surface and let go of the straw, the air moves out of the straw in one direction and the car moves in the opposite direction.

Duration
of experiment
45 Mins

Difficulty
level
High

61 Straw Fountain

Duration of experiment: 05 Mins

Difficulty level: Medium

What would you need?

Cork

Water

Bottle

Nail

Straw

What to do?

Step 1. Make a hole in the cork large enough for the straw to fit in.

Step 2. Fill half the bottle with water and cork it. Put the straw in.

Step 3. Blow into the straw and immediately move your head away.

Step 4. Water comes spurting out.

What just happened?

By blowing, you compressed the air inside the bottle, increasing the pressure. When you stopped, the compressed air expanded again, pushing the water back up the straw.

Duration of experiment: 10 Mins

Difficulty level: Low

What would you need?

Pin

Plastic bottle

Balloon

62 Balloon in a Bottle

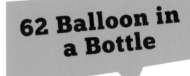

What to do?

Step 1. Put the balloon in the bottle. Cover the mouth of the bottle with the balloon.

Step 2. Try to blow the balloon. You will not be able to.

Step 3. Now poke a hole at the bottom of the bottle and try again. You can now blow the balloon.

What just happened?

Without the hole, the air inside the bottle is exerting pressure on the balloon, making it impossible to blow. Once you made a hole, the balloon was able to push the air from the bottle out to make space.

63 Floating Ball

Duration of experiment: 10 Mins

Difficulty level: Medium

What would you need?

Ping-pong ball

Bendy straw

What to do?

Step 1. Bend the straw into an L shape.

Step 2. Put the longer end of the straw in your mouth.

Step 3. Hold the ping-pong ball over the short end of the straw and blow. See your ping-pong ball levitate!

What just happened?

Moving air is at a lower pressure than still air. So, the ball is surrounded by a higher pressure. This ensures that the balloon remains over the straw.

Duration of experiment: 10 Mins

Difficulty level: Low

64 Dry Newspaper

What would you need?

Bowl half filled with water

Glass

Newspaper

What to do?

Step 1. Stuff a sheet of newspaper into the glass. Make sure it is packed tight but do not let it come all the way up to the rim of the glass.

Step 2. Turn the glass over and submerge it straight into the bowl. Do not tilt the glass.

Step 3. Hold it there for 10 seconds and take it out. Your newspaper sheet is as dry as the Sahara desert!

What just happened?

There is a layer of air between the newspaper and the water. This layer exerts pressure on the water and does not let it touch the newspaper.

Air is everywhere all the time, though we cannot see, hear or feel it. In fact, most often we don't even notice its presence. But try holding your breath for more than a minute or two and you'll definitely notice its absence!

This section deals with the various properties of air. Among many other things, you will also learn unconventional methods of inflating a balloon without touching it to your mouth.

THE AIRY GODMOTHER

Experiments
involving the properties
of Air

Duration of experiment
15 Mins

Difficulty level
Medium

65 Incredible Hoop Glider

What would you need?

Straw

Tape   Scissors

Card paper

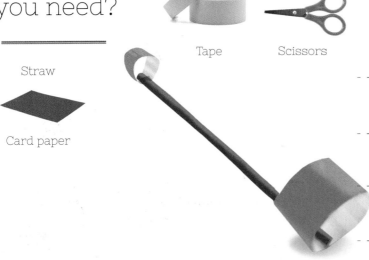

What to do?

Step 1. Cut the card paper into three strips (2.5 cm 13 cm).

Step 2. Make one large loop out of two strips.

Step 3. Make a smaller loop out of the third strip.

Step 4. Tape both the loops to the ends of the straw.

Step 5. Hold your glider by the straw, angle it upwards and launch it into the air!

What just happened?

The two loops keep the straw balanced. The large loop creates a 'drag' which keeps it airborne, and the smaller one keeps it from turning off course.

66 Obedient Smoke

Duration of experiment
15 Mins

Difficulty level
High

What would you need?

Scissors

Pencil

Cardboard tubes

Paper

Candle

Shoebox

Matchsticks

What to do?

Step 1. Place the tubes on the two edges of the shoe box lid.

- - - - - - - - - - - - - - - - - -

Step 2. Trace the outline of the tubes.

- - - - - - - - - - - - - - - - - -

Step 3. Cut out two circles in the lid of the shoe box to fit the tubes in.

- - - - - - - - - - - - - - - - - -

Step 4. Fix the tubes in the lid. These will now function as 'chimneys'.

- - - - - - - - - - - - - - - - - -

Step 5. Light the candle and place it exactly below one of the 'chimneys'.

- - - - - - - - - - - - - - - - - -

Step 6. Twist a bit of paper, light it and blow it out.

- - - - - - - - - - - - - - - - - -

Step 7. Hold the now smouldering paper over the chimney without the candle below it.

- - - - - - - - - - - - - - - - - -

Step 8. The smoke obediently comes up from the other chimney (the one with the candle under it).

- - - - - - - - - - - - - - - - - -

What just happened?

The candle uses all the oxygen in the box and therefore draws in more air from the other tube. The smoke from the paper is also drawn into the box in this manner. It then gets heated in the box and rises out of the chimney along with the warm air.

67 Self Inflating Balloon

Duration of experiment
20 Mins

Difficulty level
Medium

What would you need?

Empty bottle

Balloon

Pan

Water

What to do?

Step 1. Stretch the balloon over the mouth of the empty bottle.

Step 2. Put the bottle in the pan of hot water for a few minutes.

Step 3. You should be able to see the balloon inflating soon

What just happened?

As the air inside the bottle starts getting heated, it begins to expand. This air is trapped by the balloon, which begins stretching.

Duration of experiment
10 Mins

Difficulty level
Medium

68 Smoggy

What would you need?

Paper

Jar

Aluminium foil

Ice-cubes

Matchsticks

Water

What to do?

Step 1. Make a 'lid' for the jar with the aluminium foil.

Step 2. Take it off and wet the insides of the jar with the water.

Step 3. Put a few scraps of burning paper in the jar.

Step 4. Immediately seal the jar with aluminium foil and put the ice cubes on top. The air inside the jar will soon look smoggy.

What just happened?

The burning paper caused some of the water in the jar to evaporate. This water vapour then rose and condensed back into drops of water when it came into contact with the foil.

What would you need?

Cling wrap

Tape

Talcum powder

Shoe box

Scissors

Duration
of experiment
15 Mins

Difficulty
level
High

What just happened?

The powder takes the form of doughnut-like shapes on its way out. Because the powder moves slower than the air, it maintains its shape.

VORTICES

The scientific name for your 'smoke rings' is vortices. Vortices occur when liquids or gases spin or flow in a circular manner. Vortices usually occur in water but they sometimes occur in air.

Science around us

What to do?

Step 1. Cut off one side of the shoe box and replace it with cling wrap.

Step 2. Cut a hole on the opposite side of the box.

Step 3. Put some talcum powder in the box.

Step 4. Tap on the plastic covered side and watch the rings form!

Go Green

Though they can't walk and talk like us, plants are living things. They grow over a period of time. There are some conditions that help them grow and some that don't.

Plants also have other interesting properties that are fun to study. For example, did you know that you could grow a plant parallel to the ground? Or that you can take the 'green' out of a leaf? Learn how to in this section!

Experiments with Plants

70 Why Leaves are green

What would you need?

Duration of experiment
07 Days

Difficulty level
Low

Black chart paper   Plant   Scissors   Paper clips

What to do?

Step 1. Cover a few leaves with black chart paper.

Step 2. Put the plant where it can get plenty of sunlight.

Step 3. After a week, take the black paper off. The leaves you had covered are not as green as the others.

What just happened?

Leaves get their green colour from a substance that they produce, called 'chlorophyll'. Chlorophyll can be made only in the presence of sunlight. The leaf wrapped in chart paper did not get any sunlight.

71 Grow a Plant

Duration of experiment
03 Days

Difficulty level
Low

What would you need?

Container

Sprouts

Water

Cotton wool

What to do?

Step 1. Line the container with damp cotton.

Step 2. Place the sprouts on the damp cotton and leave it on a window sill.

Step 3. Every time the cotton dries up, dampen it again.

Step 4. The sprouts will grow in a few days.

What just happened?

You can see the sprouts giving off small roots into the cotton, and a shoot begins to grow. Plants need water and sunlight to grow.

Duration of experiment
07 Days

Difficulty level
High

72 Graft a Plant

What would you need?

Craft Knife

String

Potato plant

Modelling clay

Tomato plant

What to do?

Step 1. Pull the main stems of the potato and tomato plants together and tie them loosely with a string.

Step 2. Shave the bark till you can see the interior tubes.

Step 3. Tightly wrap string around the two shaved ends. Seal it with clay.

Step 4. After a week, cut off the old potato and old tomato plants above the wrapped part, creating a new 'pomato' plant.

What just happened?

This process is called plant 'grafting'. The new plant imbibes properties of both the old plants.

73 The Plant's Backbone

Duration of experiment
14 Days

Difficulty level
Medium

What would you need?

Black cardboard

Water

2 tsp. baking soda

Bowl

½ cup bleach

Leaves

Books

What just happened?

Leaves make food for the plant. The stem absorbs and transports the baking soda solution to the veins. When we put the leaves in bleach, all the green pigment (chlorophyll) turned white, but the baking soda in the veins didn't

Step 1. Mix two cups of warm water and baking soda in a shallow bowl.

Step 2. Submerge the leaves in this mixture.

Step 3. Leave the bowl in a sunny area for 12 days.

Step 4. Place the leaves between two pages of a book and leave it for two days.

Step 5. Mix the bleach with two cups of warm water and pour the mixture into a shallow bowl till the leaves whiten.

Step 6. Dry them and mount them on a black cardboard.

Step 7. You will be able to see the veins clearly.

Duration
of experiment

10 Days

Difficulty
level

Medium

What would you need?

Long nail

Knife

String

Water

Carrot

What to do?

Step 1. Choose a carrot that has a few leaves on its head.

Step 2. Cut about two inches from the top.

Step 3. Take help from an adult to hollow out the carrot top.

Step 4. Push the nail in horizontally and tie the string to both the ends of the nail.

Step 5. Fill the hollow with water.

Step 6. Hang your carrot with the leaves pointing downwards.

Step 7. Keep refilling the hollow every time it gets dry.

Step 8. Soon the leaves will start growing upwards, against gravity.

What just happened?

The shoot of the plant will always grow against gravity. Since the carrot is actually the root of the plant, it absorbs water and transports it to the leaves. When the leaves get enough nutrition to grow, they grow against the force of gravity.

Science around us

Why do roots always grow downward?

No one knows exactly how, but plants are able to sense gravitational force.
The root always grows in the direction of the gravitational pull, while the shoot always grows against it. This is called 'gravitropism'.

LIVE IT UP

Your body is one of the most amazing scientific miracles. Did you know that in just one day, your heart beats 100,000 times? And that if you laid out all your blood vessels from end to end they would reach about 60,000 miles? Scientists have figured out a lot about the way our body functions, but a lot still remains a mystery. Go ahead—discover more about yourself and your body in this section!

Experiments on the Human body

75 A Bird in the Cage

Duration of experiment
10 Mins

Difficulty level
Medium

What would you need?

Glue

Pencil

2 white card papers

What to do?

Step 1. Draw a cage on one card paper and a bird on the other.

Step 2. Stick both papers with the pencil in the middle.

Step 3. Hold the pencil between your hands and roll it quickly to cage the bird.

What just happened?

The eye retains images for about a second.

This is called 'persistence of vision'. When your eye sees the bird and the cage in rapid succession, both pictures get merged and it looks like the bird is in the cage.

Duration
of experiment
10 Mins

Difficulty
level
Low

What would you need?

2 card papers   Red paper   Glue   Scissors   Black marker

What to do?

Step 1. Draw a fish on the red paper. Draw an eye with the marker.

Step 2. Cut it out and glue this onto the white card paper.

Step 3. On another white card paper, draw a fishbowl.

Step 4. Take the fish card to a bright area.

Step 5. Stare at the eye of the fish for 10-15 seconds.

Step 6. Now, quickly look at the card with the fishbowl. You can see the fish in the bowl, but with a blue-green tinge!

What just happened?

The ghostly fish is called an 'afterimage'. There are colour sensitive cells at the back of your eye. When you stare at the red fish for a long time, the 'red sensitive' cells get tired of responding to red. When you look at the blank card, your eyes respond to the green and blue light that the card is reflecting, but not the red, which is why you see a blue-green ghostly fish in the bowl.

Science around us

Afterimages can be positive or negative. A positive afterimage has the same colours as the original image, whereas a negative afterimage has inverse colours (like the fish).

Duration of experiment
01 Hour

Difficulty level
High

What would you need?

90 ml water

Strawberry

Plastic containers

Sieve

Dishwashing liquid

Zip lock bag

Tweezers

¼ tsp. salt

5 ml isopropyl alcohol (available at chemists)

What to do?

Step 1. Put the isopropyl alcohol in the freezer.

Step 2. Mix the water, dishwashing liquid and salt in the plastic container.

Step 3. Put a strawberry in the zip lock bag. Remove as much air as you can to flatten it.

Step 4. Smash the strawberry with your hands till there are no chunks left.

Step 5. Pour this pulp and the solution you made earlier into another container through the sieve.

Step 6. Separate around 50-100 ml of this solution and add the isopropyl alcohol to it.

Step 7. The white layer on top of the rest of the solution is the DNA of the strawberry!

Step 8. You can remove this using tweezers.

What just happened?

All living things contain DNA. The solution you made with the dishwashing liquid and the salt acts as an extraction solution. The soap dissolves the cell membranes. The salt breaks up protein chains that hold nucleic acid together. Finally, DNA is not soluble in isopropyl alcohol, making it easy to identify.

Duration of experiment
01 Hour

Difficulty level
Medium

What would you need?

Paper

Scissors

Stapler

Pencil

What to do?

Step 1. Cut the paper to 20-30 rectangles around 15 cm x 20 cm.

Step 2. Staple them on one side.

Step 3. Start by drawing something on the last page. (E.g. A person with his hand down.)

Step 4. On the second last page, draw the exact same thing, but with a slight variation. (E.g. The person with his hand slightly raised.)

Step 5. Change the drawing a little more on the third last page. (E.g. Raise the hand even more.)

Step 6. Keep going till you eventually reach the first page.

Step 7. Now flip the pages to enjoy the illusion of motion!

What just happened?

The drawing looks like it is moving because every picture remains in the mind for a split second after it has actually disappeared. This is called 'persistence of vision'. So, when you flip them all quickly, because the previous picture is still in your mind, it merges with the current picture and gives the illusion of motion.

Duration
of experiment
10 Mins

Difficulty
level
Low

What would you need?

Food colouring

Stapler

Cotton ball

Paper

Mirror

What to do?

Step 1. Dip the cotton ball in food colouring and swipe it across your tongue.

Step 2. Punch a hole in the paper and put it on your tongue.

Step 3. Look in a mirror and count the number of bumps you can see in the hole. If there are more than 25, you are a super taster!

What just happened?

The tiny bumps on your tongue are your taste buds. There are four types of taste buds—bitter, sour, salty and sweet. The more taste buds you have, the better your sense of taste.

Almost all magic is actually just illusion that is based on various scientific principles.
This section is a neat collection of 'science tricks' with which you can bewilder, befuddle and bemuse your friends.

Confuse them with rubber bones, disappearing ink, invisible ink, vanishing water, paper loop, and more!

Got You

Science Tricks and Pranks

80 Stink it up

What would you need?

Scissors

Jar

2 tbsp household ammonia (available at grocery stores and supermarket)

20 strike-anywhere matchsticks

Duration of experiment
04 Days

Difficulty level
Medium

What to do?

Step 1. Cut the heads of the matchsticks.

Step 2. Put them in the jar and add the ammonia.

Step 3. Close the jar and swirl the contents around.

Step 4. Wait for four days and then open the jar to unleash the stench!

! The fumes from hydrogen sulphide are flammable and can be toxic. Make sure you perform the experiment in a well ventilated place and be careful.

What just happened?

The matchstick heads are made out of phosphorus sulphide. The phosphorus sulphide and ammonia react to form a nasty smelling substance called ammonium sulphide.

81 Good Juice Bad Juice

Duration
of experiment
30 Mins

Difficulty
level
Medium

What would you need?

1 tsp. red grape juice

Safety glasses

Glasses

Rubber gloves

1/2 tsp. cooking vinegar

Water

1/8 tsp. ammonia (available at supermarkets and grocery stores)

Do not try to drink ANY of the solutions created during this experiment. Use gloves while conducting the experiment, as ammonia can cause tissue damage if it comes in contact with your skin.

What to do?

Step 1. Wear the safety goggles and rubber gloves.

Step 2. In the first glass, add water and grape juice.

Step 3. In the second, add ammonia.

Step 4. In the third, add vinegar.

Step 5. Gather an audience.

Step 6. Start off with the first glass, saying that it is good juice.

Step 7. Pour it into the second glass. The juice will turn green. Say that the good juice has now turned bad.

Step 8. Finally, ask the audience to pray real hard for the juice to turn good again.

Step 9. Pour this solution into the last glass, and voila! The liquid returns to its original colour!

What just happened?

When you poured the grape juice into the ammonia, it created an alkaline solution which was green in colour. In the third glass, the acidic vinegar neutralises the alkaline solution, returning it to its original colour.

Duration
of experiment
10 Mins

Difficulty
level
Medium

82 Paper Loop

What would you need?

Scissors

7 cm x 12 cm
cardpaper

What to do?

Step 1. Fold the card lengthwise in half.

Step 2. Make 13 cuts width-wise.

Step 3. First cut from the edges towards the folded centre, then turn the paper around and cut from the centre towards the edge.

Step 4. Now, carefully open out the paper and cut along the fold. Don't cut the two sections at the edge.

Step 5. Shake the paper a little. You'll have a loop that goes over your head!

What just happened?

The secret to this trick comes from a branch of mathematics called 'topology'. It teaches that figures can be stretched without changing their area.

HIGH AND DRY

We all know that water covers a majority of the Earth's surface. We also know how important water is for our survival. In fact, 70% of our body is made up of water. One of the properties of water, that makes it very interesting to study, is known as surface tension. Surface tension is the ability of water to form a thin, skin-like membrane over its surface (like the layer that forms on top of a thick soup).

Experiments with Water

83 Coloured Ice

What would you need?

Containers

Watercolours

Water

Salt

Large tray

Difficulty level
Low

Duration of experiment
30 Mins

What to do?

Step 1. Fill different sized containers with water and put them in the freezer overnight.

- - - - - - - - - - - - - - - - -

Step 2. The next day, take the ice out in a large tray.

- - - - - - - - - - - - - - - - -

Step 3. Put some salt on the ice. Wait for a few minutes.

- - - - - - - - - - - - - - - - -

Step 4. On top of the ice blocks, put a few drops of water colour.

- - - - - - - - - - - - - - - - -

Step 5. The colour runs down the ice in rivulets, creating a fantastic display of colour!

- - - - - - - - - - - - - - - - -

What just happened?

Salt lowers the freezing point of water. So when you add it to ice, it melts at the point where the salt comes in contact with the ice. The colour runs down the ravines caused in these blocks by the salt.

84 Tornado in a Bottle

Duration of experiment
10 Mins

Difficulty level
Low

What would you need?

Dishwashing liquid   Glass jar

Glitter   Water

What to do?

Step 1. Fill 3/4th of the glass jar with water.

Step 2. Add a few drops of dishwashing liquid and some glitter.

Step 3. Put the cap on tightly.

Step 4. Quickly spin the bottle in a circular motion for a few seconds.

Step 5. Stop and look inside to see if you can see a mini tornado forming in the water.

What just happened?

Spinning the bottle in a circular motion creates a water vortex that looks like a mini tornado because of a force called the 'centripetal' force.

85 Wet Pepper

Duration of experiment
10 Mins

Difficulty level
Medium

What to do?

Step 1. Fill the bowl with water.

Step 2. Shake some pepper onto the surface of the water.

Step 3. Dip a finger in. Nothing spectacular happens.

Step 4. Put a little dishwashing liquid on your finger and dip your finger in the water again.

Step 5. Watch the pepper race to the edge of the bowl.

What would you need?

Dishwashing liquid   Bowl

Pepper   Water

What just happened?

Coating your finger with soap when you dip it in the water reduces the surface tension of the water. Therefore, the pepper spreads out.

86 Dry Hands

Duration of experiment: 10 Mins

Difficulty level: Low

What would you need?

Talcum powder

Bowl

Water

Coin

What to do?

Step 1. Drop a coin into the bowl of water.

Step 2. Try to remove it with your hand without wetting your hand. Quite impossible, isn't it?

Step 3. Sprinkle a layer of talcum powder on the surface of the water.

Step 4. You can now put your hand in and retrieve the coin without wetting your hand!

What just happened?

As soon as you put your hand in the water, it gets covered with the powder, which makes your hand waterproof.

Duration of experiment: 03 Hours

Difficulty level: Medium

87 Crystallise

What to do?

Step 1. Cut the black paper so that it lines the bottom of the pan.

Step 2. Mix the epsom salt and the water.

Step 3. Pour the salty water into the pan.

Step 4. Put the pan out in the Sun.

Step 5. After a few hours, you will see lots of crystal spikes on the paper!

What would you need?

Pan   1 tbsp. epsom salt (available at a pharmacy)

Black chart paper

Water

Scissors

What just happened?

The salt dissolves in the water when you first mix it. In the Sun, the water evaporates, leaving the crystals behind.

Duration
of experiment
30 Mins

Difficulty
level
Medium

What would you need?

 Ruler

 Stones or pebbles

 Knife

 Plastic bottle

Water

 Marker

 Sticky tape

What to do?

Step 1. Cut off the top of the bottle.

Step 2. Place some stones at the bottom of the bottle.

Step 3. Turn the top upside down and tape it to the bottle.

Step 4. Use the ruler and marker to make a scale on the bottle.

Step 5. Pour water into the bottle till it reaches the lowest mark on the scale.

Step 6. Now put it outdoors when it starts raining. Measure the rising water level.

What just happened?

The rain falls on top of the gauge and collects at the bottom, where it can be measured easily. Measure the rainfall in your gauge every time it rains. Then, try to identify what type of shower it was – short or long, heavy or light.

If you have ever touched someone or something on a dry winter morning and felt a sudden shock or current pass through, you have experienced static electricity.

Static electricity is created when small negatively charged particles (called electrons) jump from one object to another. Static is extremely fun and interesting to experiment with.

Shocking

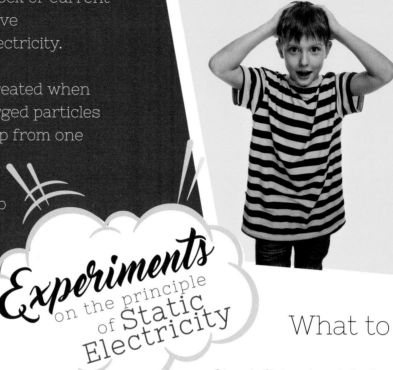

Experiments on the principle of Static Electricity

89 Holy Balloon

What would you need?

Scissors

Balloon

Plastic bag

Woollen fabric

Duration of experiment

15 Mins

Difficulty level

Medium

What to do?

Step 1. Cut out a strip from the open end of the plastic bag.

Step 2. Blow the balloon and tie it up.

Step 3. Rub the balloon with the woollen fabric for 45 seconds.

Step 4. Flatten the plastic ring and rub it with the same woollen fabric.

Step 5. Leave the band about one foot over the balloon and release it. The ring floats over the balloon, giving it a halo!

What just happened?

Rubbing the plastic and the balloon gives them both the same charge, which makes them repel each other.

90 Electroscope

What would you need?

Comb

Aluminium foil

Copper wire

Jar

Aluminium plate

What to do?

Step 1. Bend the copper wire in a 'Z' shape.

Step 2. Fold the foil and hang it on the bottom of the wire.

Step 3. Leave the top horizontal part over the top of the jar.

Step 4. Put the aluminium plate on top to hold it in place.

Step 5. Run the comb through your hair and bring it close to the jar.

Step 6. You will see the two strips of aluminium spring apart.

What just happened?

When you bring the comb close to the aluminium foil, it becomes charged. Since like charges repel, the aluminium foil leaves repel each other.

Difficulty level
High

Duration of experiment
15 Mins

---

91 Spinning Matchsticks

What would you need?

Ballon

Matchsticks

Plastic cup

2 copper coins

What to do?

Step 1. Balance one coin vertically on the other.

Step 2. Balance the matchstick horizontally on this.

Step 3. Carefully put the plastic cup over this apparatus.

Step 4. Blow up the balloon and tie it.

Step 5. Rub the balloon against your hair and bring it near the glass.

Step 6. Watch as the matchstick follows the balloon.

What just happened?

Rubbing the balloon created a negative charge in the balloon. The matchstick has a neutral charge and was attracted to the balloon, which is why it 'followed' the balloon.

Difficulty level
Medium

Duration of experiment
15 Mins

Difficulty level
Medium

Duration of experiment
15 Mins

What to do?

Step 1. Make small loops at both ends of the wire.

Step 2. Cut thin strips out of the tissue paper and push them in through one end such that equal lengths of paper stick out.

Step 3. Tape the pencil to the middle of the wire to make a handle.

Step 4. Blow up the balloon and rub it in your hair to create static.

Step 5. Hold the pencil in your hand and touch the balloon to the free end of the wire.

Step 6. Watch the 'petals' unfold.

What would you need?

Tape

Wire

Tissue Paper

Pencil

Scissors

Balloon

What just happened?

When you bring the comb close to the aluminium foil, it becomes charged. Since like charges repel, the aluminium foil leaves repel each other.

Science around us

Static is used to paint cars. To make sure a car's paint is uniform and that it will resist the high speeds, it is applied with a static charge. The metal body of the car is submerged in a substance that charges it positively and the paint is charged negatively with the paint sprayer.

Difficulty
level
Low

Duration
of experiment
10 Mins

93 Balloon Attraction

What would you need?

Woollen fabric   String   2 balloons

What to do?

Step 1. Blow up two balloons and tie strings to them.

Step 2. Hold the balloons from the strings about 3 cm apart. Notice that they are neutral.

Step 3. Rub one balloon against the woollen fabric.

Step 4. Watch as the balloons get attracted to each other.

Step 5. Now rub the other balloon to the woollen fabric as well.

Step 6. Notice how they repel each other.

What just happened?

Before rubbing the balloon, both had neutral charges and were neither attracted to nor repelled by each other. When you rubbed only one balloon, it got charged. The second balloon, however, was still neutral, so they were attracted to each other. However, when both balloons were rubbed, both of them got equal charges and thus repelled each other.

79

Difficulty
level
Low

Duration
of experiment
10 Mins

What would you need?

Doorknob

Small pieces of dry cereal

Thread

Science around us

Photocopy machines use static electricity
It's true! In copy machines more ink gets attracted to darker areas because of static. Copy machines use the charge to apply ink only in the areas where the paper to be copied is darker and not where the paper is white.

What to do?

Step 1. Tie a piece of cereal to one end of a string.

Step 2. Hang the string from a metal doorknob.

Step 3. Comb your hair briskly with a dry comb around 20 times.

Step 4. Now bring the comb close to the cereal. It will swing to touch the comb.

Step 5. Wait for a few seconds till it jumps away.

Step 6. Now every time you try to touch it, it will move away.

Step 7. You can control the cereal in this way, just like a remote control car!

What just happened?

When you combed your hair, the comb got negatively charged. Being neutral, the cereal jumped to the comb. As soon as this happened, negative electrons got transferred from the comb to the cereal. Once this happened, both objects had the negative charge and repelled each other.

Almost everything that we take for granted today runs on electricity. The TV, computer, phone, lights and fans—EVERYTHING works because of electricity. Electricity is nothing but a constant flow of electrons. In this section, you will learn a lot about the elementary principles behind electricity. Remember that electricity can be dangerous. Perform all these experiments only under adult supervision.

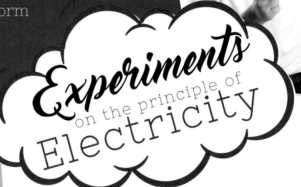

Current Affairs

Experiments on the principle of Electricity

95 Conductor of Electricity

What would you need?

Battery

Clip

Tape

Flashlight bulb

Scissors

Coin

Aluminium foil

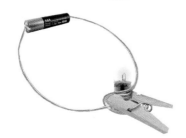

Duration
of experiment
10 Mins
Difficulty
level
High

What to do?

Step 1. Cut the aluminium foil to make two 60 cm strips.

- - - - - - - - - - - - - - - - - - -

Step 2. Tape one end of both strips to the battery. Wrap the other end around the base of the bulb.

- - - - - - - - - - - - - - - - - - -

Step 3. Use the clip to hold it in place.

- - - - - - - - - - - - - - - - - - -

Step 4. Now, touch the base of the bulb to the coin. See the bulb light up!

- - - - - - - - - - - - - - - - - - -

What just happened?

Some materials allow electricity to pass through them easily and some do not. The coin completes the circuit by allowing electricity to pass through it.

96 Magnetic Circuit

Duration of experiment
10 Mins

Difficulty level
Medium

What would you need?

4 ft. copper wire

Bar magnet

Paper cutter

Compass

What just happened?

Placing a wire across a moving magnetic field causes a current to flow through the wire. Such a path is called a circuit.

What to do?

Step 1. Scrape the insulation from both ends of the wire.

Step 2. Leave a foot on each end and coil the middle around four fingers.

Step 3. Join both ends of the wire.

Step 4. Move the magnet in and out of the coil.

Step 5. Hold the compass near the coil. The needle of the compass jiggles.

Science around us

How do electric switches work? Switches work in a similar manner to the circuits you just made. When the switch is in an 'on' position, it completes the circuit. That is how electrons flow and whatever appliance you are switching 'on' works. On the other hand, in an 'off' position, the circuit is broken. This causes the flow of electrons to stop and the appliance to stop working.

97 Lighten Up

What would you need?

Tape

5 inch wire

Paper cutter

Flashlight bulb

Battery

Difficulty level
High

Duration of experiment
20 Mins

What to do?

Step 1. Scrape the insulation off both ends of the wire.

Step 2. Curl one end of the wire tightly around the grooves at the base of the bulb.

Step 3. Shape the other end into a coil.

Step 4. Tape the coil to the bottom of a dry cell.

Step 5. Tape the rest of the wire to the cell such that the base of the bulb can touch the positive terminal of the battery.

What just happened?

By connecting the positive and negative terminals of the battery, you completed the circuit, causing electricity to flow. This electric power lit up the bulb.

Duration of experiment
30 Mins

Difficulty level
High

What to do?

Step 1. Remove half an inch of the insulation from each end of all three wires.

Step 2. Tape one end of one of the wires to the positive terminal of the battery.
Tape the other end to a paper clip.

Step 3. Use a thumbtack to secure the end of that paper clip to the cardboard.

Step 4. Wrap one end of another wire to the side of the light bulb and the other end to the negative terminal of the battery.

Step 5. Wrap one end of the third wire around the negative terminal of the battery and place the other end near the paper clip.

Step 6. Touch the paper clip to the end of the third wire to see the bulb light up.
You can now use the paper clip as a switch to turn the bulb on and off.

What just happened?

All the materials used in the circuit are good conductors of electricity as they allow electrons to flow freely through them. This free flow of electrons provides energy, which lights up the bulb.

What would you need?

3 wires   Thumbtack

1 battery (4.5 volt)   Tape   Light bulb

Cardboard   1 paper clip

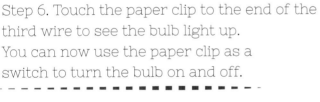

Duration
of experiment
10 Mins

Difficulty
level
High

What to do?

Step 1. Tape the D-sized batteries together, with the positive end of one battery touching the negative end of the other.

Step 2. Cut the tube to a height that fits comfortably in the glass jar.

Step 3. Tape one positive and one negative alligator clip to one end of the tube.

Step 4. Carefully place a mechanical pencil lead between the two alligator clips.

Step 5. Place the glass jar over the top of the tube stand and the plate under it, as shown.

Step 6. Touch the other ends of the alligator clips to the ends of the battery.

Step 7. In a moment, the pencil lead begins to glow.

What would you need?

0.5 mm pencil lead

Alligator clips

Electric tape

Cardboard tube

Aluminium plate

Glass jar

8 D-sized batteries

What just happened?

You completed the circuit by touching the ends of the alligator clips to the battery. This flow of electricity heats the pencil lead to an incredible temperature, which makes it glow and let out smoke.

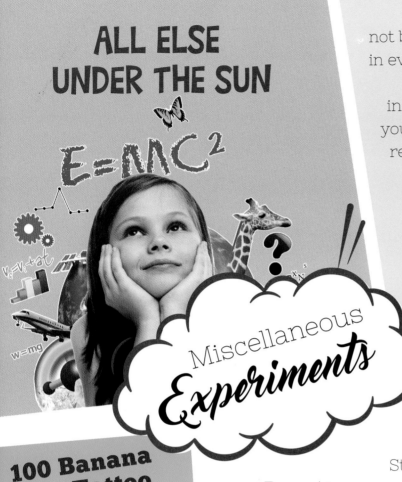

ALL ELSE UNDER THE SUN

$E = MC^2$

Miscellaneous Experiments

Though you may not believe it, science is present in everything around you. From the space stations in outer space to the fact that you are sitting here right now, reading this book – there is a scientific explanation for everything – well, almost everything. This section is based on no theme in particular, but is a miscellaneous collection of experiments that did not fit into any other section.

100 Banana Tattoo

What would you need?

Toothpick

Banana

Paper

Pencil

Duration of experiment
30 Mins

Difficulty level
Low

What to do?

Step 1. Draw any tattoo shape on the paper.

- - - - - - - - - - - - - - - - - - - -

Step 2. Place the paper on the banana and trace the shape with the toothpick. Make sure that the toothpick pierces the banana skin.

- - - - - - - - - - - - - - - - - - - -

Step 3. Wait for half an hour. You now have a tattooed banana!

- - - - - - - - - - - - - - - - - - - -

What just happened?

When the peel of the banana is cut or bruised, an enzyme called 'polyphenol oxidase' is released. This reacts with air, causing the brown colour on it.

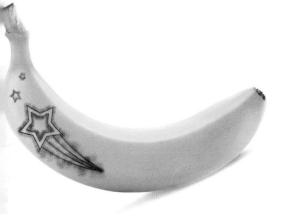

Duration of experiment **24 Hours**

Difficulty level High

Rolling pin　　Sieve　　Newspaper　　Blender　　Water　　Cloth　　2 planks of wood

What to do?

Step 1. Put the newspaper in the blender. Add water and blend it till it is a nice, smooth paste.

- - - - - - - - - - - - - - - -

Step 2. Pour this paste through the sieve to drain out the water.

- - - - - - - - - - - - - - - -

Step 3. Put the pulp onto the cloth and flatten it with a rolling pin.

- - - - - - - - - - - - - - - -

Step 4. Cover the top of the paper with another cloth.

- - - - - - - - - - - - - - - -

Step 5. Put the cloth with the paper between two planks of wood.

- - - - - - - - - - - - - - - -

Step 6. Stand on it to flatten it out.
Step 7. Let it dry overnight. You can now enjoy your recycled paper.

- - - - - - - - - - - - - - - -

What just happened?

Paper is made up of long fibres from wood or vegetable products. While recycling paper, you separated these fibres and rearranged them. Every time you recycle paper the fibres get shorter, which limits the number of times the same paper can be recycled.

How is paper recycled on a large scale?

The basic process behind recycling is the same in the large plants as your homemade paper. The only difference is in the machines used. Huge mixers are used to create the slurry and huge rollers are then used to flatten them out.

OTHER TITLES IN THIS SERIES

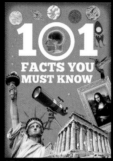

978-93-86316-11-0

978-93-86316-08-0

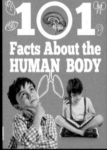

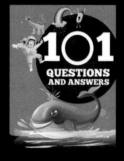

978-93-86316-09-7

978-93-81607-39-8

978-93-86316-10-3

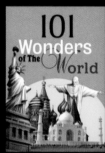

978-93-80069-59-3

978-93-80069-87-6

978-93-86316-07-3

978-93-80070-78-0

978-93-80069-85-2

978-93-80069-90-6

978-93-80069-57-9

978-93-80070-76-6

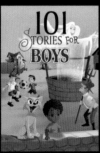

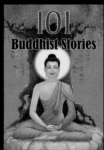

978-93-80070-75-9

978-93-80070-77-3

978-93-80069-58-6

978-93-81607-35-0